With the Fish

by Susan McCloskey

illustrated by Richard Hull

Scott Foresman

Editorial Offices: Glenview, Illinois • New York, New York
Sales Offices: Reading, Massachusetts • Duluth, Georgia
Glenview, Illinois • Carrollton, Texas • Menlo Park, California

Pam is happy.

Why?

She saw green fish.

Here they are!

Tim is happy.

Why?

He saw yellow fish.

Here they are!

Max and Rick are happy.

Why?

They saw red fish.

Here they are.

Jan is happy.

Why?

She saw purple fish.

Can you see the fish?

8